Where Do You Hurt?

Where Do You Hide?

By Randy Walter

Where Do You Hurt? Were Do You Hide?

Copyright © 2016 by Shiloh Ministries, Inc.

ISBN 978-0-9890789-2-4

Published by Shiloh Ministries, Inc., in February, 2016

Unless otherwise specified, all Scriptures are taken from the *New King James Version*. Copyright © 1982 by Thomas Nelson, Inc. Used by permission. All rights reserved.

Scripture quotations marked "AMP" are taken from the *Amplified® Bible*, Copyright © 1954, 1958, 1962, 1964, 1965, 1987 by The Lockman Foundation. Used by permission.

Scripture quotations marked "ESV" are from *The Holy Bible, English Standard Version®* (ESV®), copyright © 2001 by Crossway, a publishing ministry of Good News Publishers. Used by permission. All rights reserved.

Scripture quotations marked "GW" are taken from *GOD'S WORD®*, © 1995 God's Word to the Nations. Used by permission of Baker Publishing Group.

Scripture quotations marked "NASB" are taken from the *New American Standard Bible®*, Copyright © 1960, 1962, 1963, 1968, 1971, 1972, 1973, 1975, 1977, 1995 by The Lockman Foundation. Used by permission.

Scripture quotations marked "NIV" are taken from the *Holy Bible, New International Version®*. Copyright © 1973, 1978, 1984 by International Bible Society. Used by permission of Zondervan. All rights reserved.

Printed in the United States of America.

Where Do
You Hurt?

Where Do
You Hide?

This Book Belongs to

Randy & Lu Ann

Presented by

Randy & Barbara

We pray this blesses you!

Other Shiloh Books

The Rehearsal or Living Life Live – 48-page booklet recounts the tests and breakthroughs when God said, "Stop rehearsing the future."
$7 each *(includes shipping)*

Things Hoped For – 25 years of prophetic wisdom and encounters with God – two books in one – 304 pages. Readers are saying—

"It is the most profoundly faith-building book I have ever read."

"It was delightfully refreshing, enlightening, and very sobering."

"...a good book to purchase for people who are struggling with their Christian walk."

"...an honest portrayal of the walk of faith."

"Excellent resource for intercessory prayer..."

$15 each *(includes shipping)*

Timeless Wisdom series of messages recorded as they were received from the Lord – 48 pages each on three different themes.

$10 for three-booklet set *(includes shipping)*

Kingdom Living

Prosperous Living

Revival Living

Send checks to:
Shiloh Ministries, 209 West St., Berlin, MD 21811
ThingsHopedFor@comcast.net

Where Do
You Hurt?

Where Do
You Hide?

Contents

Randy & Barbara's Ministry Activities

Intercession and home meetings

Books and speaking

Chapter 1

Why Do We Hide?

When I was in my early teens, the youth fellowship in our church conducted a car wash to collect money for a baptismal font in the new sanctuary. After my name was nominated as event chairman, the snickers around the room told the story. It wasn't an acknowledgement of ability, it was meant as a joke.

It was an echo of my misery from the fourth grade. When the teacher questioned students about our homework assignment, the same snickering erupted whenever she called my name. It was a foregone conclusion that I would not know the answer. I was the class dummy.

So I never volunteered for anything. I hid from everything. Being nominated to chair the car wash put a familiar knot in my stomach. To the other kids, it seemed like such a funny idea that no other names were suggested, and I was selected.

Somehow, I took the assignment seriously. We would

need posters to announce the fundraiser. The first place I approached was a department store on the highway. It was obvious by the manager's accent and stylish suit that he was from New York. He was stern and all business as I asked to put up a notice in his front window.

Company policy prohibited use of handmade posters, he responded. Pausing as he observed my easy submission and crestfallen expression, he suggested that the store could print a poster. After a phone call to someone in the basement, he sent me downstairs to the print shop. There, a friendly man in a leather apron pried the details out of me, arranged type in a galley, and printed a proof. It was professional and fabulous. I was thrilled.

Then he asked how many I would like for posting in other businesses. "Twenty," I said, wondering if I were being greedy. He happily complied and in a few minutes, I had enough of these large placards to display where everyone would see them. It was God's favor at work in my life.

The car wash was a huge success, raising more money than any other fundraiser our youth group ever held. The joke was no longer on me but on the kids who thought they could humiliate someone who hid from leadership. In my adult years, whenever I've been tempted to shrink from an assignment that seemed too difficult, I have gained confidence by thinking back to that car wash.

WHY DO WE HIDE?

Hiding: What causes it? What are its negative ramifications? How do we recognize it? How do we come out of it?

Chapter 1 – Why Do We Hide?

We hide because we hurt.

"Hide from what? I'm not hiding," most of us think. Suppose "hiding" were defined as failing to place our whole confidence in God? It would be the condition of fallen man.

The first incidence of hiding was in the Garden of Eden. Adam and Eve hid themselves from God.

"So when the woman saw that the tree was good for food, that it was pleasant to the eyes, and a tree desirable to make one wise, she took of its fruit and ate. She also gave to her husband with her, and he ate. Then the eyes of both of them were opened, and they knew that they were naked; and they sewed fig leaves together and made themselves coverings.

"And they heard the sound of the Lord God walking in the garden in the cool of the day, and Adam and his wife hid themselves from the presence of the Lord God among the trees of the garden.

"Then the Lord God called to Adam and said to him, 'Where are you?'

"So he said, 'I heard Your voice in the garden, and I was afraid because I was naked; and I hid myself'" (Genesis 3:6-10).

They were afraid because they were naked. It wasn't only an awareness that they were without clothing, which they had never worn. They perceived that the mantle of God's glory which had covered them was gone. Now their flesh had to provide protection. They recognized nakedness as vulnerability, became afraid, and hid. Men have been trying to hide from God ever since.

Where Do You Hurt? Where Do You Hide?

Think of the height from which the first man and woman fell. They had walked and talked with God face to face. They experienced daily intimacy with Him and trusted Him without reservation. They were immortal and knew no fear. All this was lost in a fateful instant.

The serpent made Eve believe God was holding out on her and Adam. "Did God *really* say you couldn't eat everything in the garden?" he asked. Then he lied, "You won't die if you do, but you will know everything God knows and be like Him."

Satan tempted her with envy and self-seeking, which produce rebellion and every evil thing (see James 3:16). With the knowledge of good and evil came the realization that Adam and Eve surrendered their authority and forfeited the intimacy they had known with God. They exchanged life for death. Imagine the agony and shame of their new reality! When they hid from God, they were trying to hide from their pain. They hid because they hurt.

After the Fall, they and their descendants lived in a world which rapidly became like the one we know today. Corruption and hiding from God increased with every generation. Hiding feeds shame, fear and an orphan mind-set.

How could men, who were created in God's image to have a relationship with Him, end up feeling like orphans? My wife, Barbara, and I asked the Lord that question, and He replied:

"It came in when man developed a sense of himself separate from Me. Sin divided us and gave him a different

4

Chapter 1 – Why Do We Hide?

identity. At the beginning, we were one. After the Fall, man started creating himself and he opened the door to thinking like an orphan.

"Ever since, man has tried to develop his own identity. The more focused he is on himself, the less open and aware he is of Me. Once, we processed everything together. Now, he tries to placate Me rather than receive Me. He still hides in an attempt to conceal his sin."

Cain tried to hide the killing of his brother Abel by asking God, **"Am I my brother's keeper?"** God had already warned him that **"sin lies at the door. And its desire is for you, but you should rule over it"** (Genesis 4:7).

Sin separates us from God, and makes us believe we can hide ourselves and what we do from Him.

"'Can anyone hide himself in secret places, so I shall not see him?' says the Lord; 'Do I not fill heaven and earth?' says the Lord" (Jeremiah 23:24).

Yet men try to conceal themselves from God anyway. The Bible contains many accounts in which men have run from His will in an attempt to avoid His destiny for their lives. Jonah's story is the most familiar.

JONAH

God told the prophet Jonah to go and preach repentance to Nineveh, a large, wicked city comparable to Sodom and Gomorrah. Instead of obeying, Jonah tried to hide by boarding a ship bound in the opposite direction. "You can run but you can't hide" was never more appropriate than for Jonah.

Where Do You Hurt? Where Do You Hide?

Perhaps Jonah was offended because God offered the evil Ninevites an opportunity to redeem themselves. Jonah looked down on the Ninevites with disdain, possibly even bitterness. Nineveh was the capital city of the mighty Assyrian Empire, whose kings were merciless warlords that raided the homeland of God's people. Jonah's family could have been among their victims.

Jonah might have resembled the Pharisee of Jesus' parable, related in Luke 18:9-14. The Pharisee and a tax collector prayed in the temple. The proud Pharisee looked down on the lowly tax collector and thanked God that he wasn't like him. The tax collector humbled himself and asked God for mercy, and was justified.

Jesus directed this comparison toward those who, like the Pharisee, **"trusted in themselves that they were righteous, and despised others."**

TRUE REPENTANCE

The ship Jonah boarded was caught in a terrific storm and about to capsize. Jonah told the sailors it was because of him, and to throw him overboard. When they did, the sea calmed. For millennia, Jonah's name would become synonymous with "jinx."

Jonah was so opposed to doing God's assignment that he would rather have died. He was swallowed by a "great fish" and remained in its belly three days and nights until he acknowledged the Lord and committed himself to obedience.

Put back on dry land, Jonah went to Nineveh and declared that God was about to destroy the city. Its inhabitants listened, fasted, and repented in sackcloth and ashes, from the king to the least of his subjects. Even their herds of animals ate and drank nothing, and were covered with sackcloth. And God relented from the destruction He said He would bring upon the city.

Despite Jonah's indignation over mercy being shown to these sinful people, he fulfilled God's destiny for his life. The Old Testament book bearing his name is a model for repentance. It is read each year on Yom Kippur, the Day of Atonement, by Jews whose tradition holds that Jonah was the boy Elijah brought back to life (I Kings 17:17-23). As a result, Jonah is believed to have shared Elijah's temperament, especially a desire for strict judgment.

Jonah was trying to hide his pain at the thought that those sinners might be made equal to him in God's sight. Is Jonah's judgment comparable to the way some Christians today respond to people involved in homosexuality, abortion, pop culture, divergent political values, or different churches and denominations?

GIDEON, JOB, DAVID

When God sent His Angel to greet Gideon as a **"mighty man of valor,"** this was more than a salutation. It was a prophetic proclamation. To conceal the wheat he had threshed from Midianite raiders, Gideon was hiding with it in the winepress.

The Midianites triggered great fear. For seven years, like swarms of locusts which could not be numbered, they destroyed Israel's crops and herds, leaving no sustenance

behind. When the Angel declared, **"The Lord is with you...
Go in this might of yours, and you shall save Israel from the
hand of the Midianites"** (Judges 6:11, 14), Gideon responded
with the equivalent of, "Who, *me?*"

But God worked on his behalf. As it turned out, the Midianites were afraid of Gideon. When he and his 300 men surrounded their camp, the raiders fell into confusion, turned on
each other, then ran. Gideon led his army to a great victory,
executed the enemy kings, and became ruler over Israel.

Job lived during the time of the patriarchs. We think of
him as God's champion who silenced the accusations of Satan
and modeled faithfulness under extreme adversity. But Job,
also, was tempted to hide from God.

In Job 13:20-21 (NIV), he said, **"Only grant me these two
things, God, and then I will not hide from You: Withdraw Your
hand far from me, and stop frightening me with Your terrors."**

After David was anointed Israel's next king, he had to
hide from Saul. On the run, he pretended to be insane to disguise himself before the king of Gath, whom he feared.

Even Peter, one of Jesus' inner circle, concealed his identity by denying Jesus after He was arrested.

These heroes of the Bible overcame hiding by trusting
God, fulfilling His destiny for their lives, and affecting countless people for generations to come. We can too.

We might think we're protecting our emotions or lives by
hiding our true selves. In reality, we deny God to others by hiding from the identity and the destiny for which He created us.

Chapter 2

How Do We Hide?

Jonah tried to hide by running from God. Gideon was hiding from his enemies when the Angel of the Lord greeted him. Job said he would not hide if God stopped frightening him. David ran from Saul and feigned being crazy. And Peter denied who he was.

How do *we* hide? It is futile to hide from God physically, but we can still do it emotionally.

My wife Barbara and I are often approached by people seeking advice. The Lord told us not to ask what they have or have not done, but to ask, "Where do you hurt? Where do you hide?" I also began to ask myself that question.

FEAR OF BEING KNOWN

One couple who requested our help had no stability, frequently moving from place to place and job to job. Even as they struggled financially, they strove to be recognized as ministry leaders. When we prayed about what to say to them, the Lord called this "being flighty" due to "fear of being known." He told us:

"At first, recognition is fulfilling. But soon after that need is met, recognition can lead to fear. Rejection seems to hide behind every form of intimacy. Running is a way to avoid it.

"All this is rooted in shame, and shame is one of the most unteachable spirits. It agrees but does not learn, due to fear of exposure. Its style is to endear but never to commit, and its fruit is the very thing the person is trying to avoid – rejection.

"To maintain its façade, shame uses dishonesty until that person no longer knows what is real. It blames and hides when the things it wants are out of reach. The longview of being flighty is desolation and self-destruction.

"Fear of being known is the biggest insecurity of all. It means you don't think you can trust anyone, so you hold everybody at bay, and then you feel lonely. Worst of all, not being able to trust anyone includes Me."

THE MEANING OF "HIDING"

What comes to mind when you think of "hiding"? Going undercover? Taking another name to avoid the threat of harm or persecution? Trying to conceal your location, like the apostles hiding from the Jews after Jesus' Crucifixion?

"Hiding" is an attempt to obscure something. The opposite is to reveal or confess. One of the meanings of "occult" is to be hidden, referring to secret knowledge and practices.

Chapter 2 – How Do We Hide?

Hiding is not just when you place yourself off limits to others. It can be done by finding your identity in an inappropriate place.

Do you know someone who identifies so strongly with a cause or another person that it becomes the reason for his existence? He is hiding his real self behind something or someone else. Name-dropping is one way to do this – mentioning well-known people to impress others, inferring that a relationship exists where it does not.

A Christian does not hide his true identity because his identity has been transformed. He is no longer who he once was. Surrendering his life to Jesus is like trading in an old car for a new one. He isn't hiding his identity because that person does not exist anymore.

In II Corinthians 5:17, Paul wrote, **"Therefore, if anyone is in Christ, he is a new creation; old things have passed away; behold, all things have become new."**

Paul told the Colossians to **"put off the old man with his deeds,"** and to **"put on the new man…"** (Colossians 3:9-10).

HIDING BEHIND RELIGION

Christianity seeks to transform rather than conceal the identity of its adherents. However, it is possible to hide behind a religious system. That is how Jesus regarded the scribes and Pharisees. He told the people to obey what they said but not to be like them, because **"they say, and do not do"** (Matthew 23:3). The scribes and Pharisees used their authority for personal gain. To ensure their position, they mercilessly subjected the people to the rigor of the Law.

Where Do You Hurt? Where Do You Hide?

The thought that I could be hiding behind a spiritual façade never occurred to me until one morning in church. I had been in a conspicuous public ministry for 20 years. It was a demanding position, and I thought I was giving God my best. So it came as a shock when, sitting smugly in a worship service, I heard a quiet voice whisper in my spirit, "You're hiding in here."

I had been more concerned with appearance and approval from men than with total obedience. I was doing part of what God assigned to me, but hiding from other things He told me to do. I wasn't much different from Jonah, except I was trying to hide in God's house behind a pretense of works.

I could see that I was like the scribes and Pharisees who loved greetings in the marketplace, the best places at feasts and the best seats in the synagogues. Jesus said what they did was to be seen by men, and called them "hypocrites." They could not hide their greed and indifference from Him.

RECOGNITION

When I was born again, I left my old life behind and was unsure of my new identity. So I used my first assignment from the Lord to try to impress people.

He called me to start a Christian newspaper through our area's Christian radio station. I had entered the journalism profession at the age of 18, and this was right up my alley.

The newspaper was called *Maranatha Manna.* I loved being the "*Manna* man." Every year, I would grab Barbara and several bundles of papers and go to the National Religious Broadcasters' annual convention in Washington, D.C. I was certain my publication was going to bring me fame and ignite the fire of revival.

One year, in a front page article, I pasted a correction in the wrong place so there was a repeated paragraph. It may not have been that conspicuous to others (if they even read it), but I was mortified. Most people would have gotten over it quickly; I plunged into two days of shock and depression. I had been looking for recognition. How could I impress anyone when I made a mistake?

I thought I was going to save the world. In my home office, I worked late into the night, usually seven days a week, thinking I was pleasing God while ignoring my family. I used the *Manna* as a place to hide from personal responsibility, even though I was serious about it as a ministry.

God finally intervened when my office was moved 35 miles away to the radio station, and I was directed to keep regular hours. After that, I left my work at the office. When I was home, I could give Barbara my full attention.

HIDING BEHIND KNOWLEDGE

"Now concerning things offered to idols: We know that we all have knowledge. Knowledge puffs up, but love edifies" (I Corinthians 8:1).

Paul was warning believers against exercising their liberty at the expense of the weak. Knowing false gods are nothing, a person might in good conscience eat food sacrificed to an idol, yet suffer no harm. But someone susceptible to idolatry might see him do that and be encouraged to defile

Where Do You Hurt? Where Do You Hide?

himself. Thus the mature person's knowledge becomes arrogance if it causes the feeble to stumble.

"Knowledge puffs up, but love edifies" has a much broader application. We can hide behind knowledge. Wrote English philosopher Thomas Hobbes, "Knowledge is power." It can breed contempt whenever someone else knows something we don't, and make us feel self-sufficient. Knowledge can cause us to hide from God's love and calling.

In the West, we have limitless resources for Christian living and ministry – from study aids to symposiums. But attending one conference after another does no good if we don't put that knowledge into practice. We run the risk of substituting knowledge for our identity so people only see what we know and not who we are. That, too, is hiding behind knowledge.

Paul warned against fraudulent believers who were **"always learning and never able to come to the knowledge of the truth"** (II Timothy 3:7). Without applying what we are taught, it's easy to be full of ourselves when we acquire knowledge. God can't fill us until we empty ourselves of ourselves.

Of course, all knowledge is not bad. Proverbs 9:10 says, **"The fear of the Lord is the beginning of wisdom, and the knowledge of the Holy One is understanding."** Knowledge itself is not the problem, but how it is viewed and used.

TAKING GOD'S NAME IN VAIN

Growing up in a churchgoing family, I was instructed that taking the Lord's name in vain was when "God" or "Jesus

Chapter 2 – How Do We Hide?

Christ" was used as an expletive. Most people who do that don't know the One whose name they are using. The word "vain" implies futility and a lack of respect.

I have corrected offenders without showing any compassion for their ignorance or concern for their souls. Even when I spoke with authority, I was self-righteously hiding behind my faith. Mine was a worse way to take the Lord's name in vain: I wore His identity without reflecting His character. The real issue wasn't their language but my arrogance.

We don't think of hiding as something done to draw attention to ourselves, but the most vain way of hiding behind knowledge is when Christians preach at each other to show off. We've all heard it and many of us have done it. To this day, I can easily slip into that bad habit if I'm not careful.

This is more than self-indulgence; it can be a mask to conceal the sinful part of our nature by spouting truths without personal conviction. It is a show intended to impress. Scripture endorses preaching as a way to win the lost, not believers preaching at each other to boast of their knowledge.

The opposite of hiding behind preaching is letting the light of Christ shine through us. Jesus encouraged this when He said, **"You are the light of the world. A city that is set on a hill cannot be hidden. Nor do they light a lamp and put it under a basket, but on a lampstand, and it gives light to all who are in the house. Let your light so shine before men, that they may see your good works and glorify your Father in heaven"** (Matthew 5:14-16).

Where Do You Hurt? Where Do You Hide?

The Church itself can be the basket under which our light is hidden. It is possible for congregations to hide in their buildings and still expect light to shine in their communities. When Jesus said to "let your light so shine before men," He meant for us to shine before all people, not just believers.

From What/Whom
Do We Hide?

Whenever we hide, we are ultimately attempting to hide from God. As in a game of hide and seek, we say to Him, "I know where I am but You don't."

We think we're hiding from what has or might hurt us, so we don't see it as backsliding. But when we're hiding, are we giving God our best?

Typically, we don't think of hiding as avoiding our spiritual calling or neglecting God's assignment for us. But Barbara and I have talked to people who say, "I'm just waiting for God to show me what my ministry is." Meanwhile, they're doing nothing. In fact, they are hiding from His will and blaming Him for the delay. If God hasn't given them a specific assignment, the Bible is full of ministry instructions that everyone is called to follow until He does.

We can also hide from other people. We don't want them

to see the things that embarrass us – our failures, character flaws and inadequacies. Bluff and bluster replace honesty and accountability. We become self-conscious and not God-confident. Fear of man makes any situation all about us and not what God can do through us.

We can hide from leadership and/or from paying the price for it. And if we hide from being known, we are like the unstable couple Barbara and I advised. When the Lord was telling us about fear of being known, He said:

"Hiding by keeping your fine qualities to yourself is an escalated form of selfishness. That is the deeper meaning of putting your light under a basket – much more than just failing to be evangelical.

"I made every person with the potential to be a gift to those around him. By not being generous with yourself out of fear, you undermine My purpose for your existence. This is the pitfall of fearing the rejection of man. Fear causes everyone to suffer loss."

HIDING FROM GOD

"If you hide from God, wisdom will hide from you," He showed me. When we hide from God, we are hiding from His goodness. Romans 2:4 says the goodness of God brings a man to repentance. We are to be containers of His character and conductors of His power. When we hide, we can actually keep others from being saved.

Many of us know people who appear to have good hearts, yet they live in defiance of God's commands. Despite the goodness they seem to possess, they are closed to Him.

18

Chapter 3 – From What/Whom Do We Hide?

Even if they are willing to talk about the Lord, there is no desire to learn about or obey Him. It's very sad to watch them pay the price of their rebellion, and to realize they may not change. How easy it is to label them "lost" without asking ourselves where they hurt and what makes them hide.

Hiding from God is like erecting a NO TRESPASSING sign to protect the parts of us that we refuse to surrender. We don't want Him or others to see them – as if we could outwit the One who **"searches all hearts and understands all the intent of the thoughts"** (I Chronicles 28:9).

He knows us better than we know ourselves. He still loves us with an everlasting love. And His purpose is to do us good and not harm. Rather than posting parts of ourselves OFF LIMITS to God, our challenge is learning to trust Him with every aspect of who we are.

DOING THINGS OUR WAY

Perhaps you, like me, quote Luke's statement in Acts 17:28, **"for in Him we live and move and have our being."** And yet how often do we do things alone without asking for God's help? Even if we aren't doing anything wrong and have nothing to conceal from Him, excluding God from our activities is really a demonstration of pride.

Perhaps that is why, once when I asked Him to take care of a concern, He responded, "The problem isn't the problem. The problem is you."

If we're undertaking something by ourselves, even if out of obedience, it is still secretive, as if done in darkness rather than in His light. We forget that in our weakness (inability, sickness, human limitations), He wants to demonstrate His strength. Refusing to allow His power to be revealed through us is like trying to hide our imperfection, ignorance and helplessness. Whenever we take credit for our gifts and achievements, we not only hide from Him but hide Him from others.

We also try to hide by ignoring the need to revere God. Jesus confronted the scribes and Pharisees for their superficial acknowledgement (Matthew 15:8-9). Calling them "hypocrites," He quoted the words of Isaiah 29:13, **"These people draw near to Me with their mouth, and honor Me with their lips, but their heart is far from Me. And in vain they worship Me, teaching as doctrines the commandments of men."**

A similar situation occurred in Malachi 1:6. God upbraided the people for expecting Him not to notice when they offered sick and blemished sacrifices. **"Where is My reverence?"** He asked.

THE WAY I WROTE

When new management came to the radio station which published the *Manna*, the vision changed from doing a newspaper to more of a feature magazine. In that shift I was told, "The readers want to hear *your* voice. No more interviews with other people. We want to know what *you* think."

That was totally opposite from what I practiced as a journalist. I didn't know it at the time, but I was hiding behind the way I wrote. My goal was to make the reader feel he had actually met the person I interviewed. By featuring other people, I kept myself from scrutiny.

Suddenly I was confronted by a need to be conspicuous.

Chapter 3 - From What/Whom Do We Hide?

I was trying to be anonymous. Now I had to take off the cloak of invisibility by being candid and vulnerable. I had not recognized the security I drew from hiding behind my writing. After four decades of interviewing others, now I was to be the subject of what I wrote.

EXPOSING MY INNER MAN

When the Lord told Barbara and me we would write a book as a result of her long-running "Things Hoped For" column in the *Manna*, it was hard for me to come to terms with its format. At first, I thought it would be the best of her columns, or a series of teachings based on them, or some other expression that left me out of the middle.

Barbara's style is so different from how I wrote. She makes herself totally transparent, revealing her struggles, doubts and fears in a way people can identify with. So many times I heard from readers that her column was the first thing they looked for in the paper. I worked long days to write, typeset, edit and produce an entire newspaper each month. But when we were introduced to people, they immediately gravitated to Barbara and said how much her column meant to them. Then, almost as a afterthought, they turned to me and said, "You must be Randy. Good job on the paper."

I had been hiding behind the written page so people could not see me. It was my way of not being known. Shame still told me I had things to conceal from others to avoid rejection and ridicule. I didn't mind people finding out things about my past if it made me look good in the present, but I was reluctant to be truly open. If they really knew me, I thought, they wouldn't like me.

Where Do You Hurt? Where Do You Hide?

The book you are reading is evidence that God is healing me of the compulsion to hide who I am. Instead of sharing other people's stories, I write my own.

This shows the power of John's statement in Revelation 12:11, **"And they overcame him** (Satan) **by the blood of the Lamb and by the word of their testimony..."**

Chapter 4

Where Do We Hide?

Hiding is demonic. Demons try to hide where and what they are.

Men try to hide from God in the world that accommodates their fears. It's the only place dark enough that they think He won't see them. John wrote that men **"loved darkness instead of light because their deeds were evil. Everyone who does evil hates the light, and will not come into the light for fear that their deeds will be exposed"** (John 3:19-20 NIV).

Like chameleons, men act as the world acts in order to conceal themselves. And the world accepts its own by telling them it's okay to ignore God. Repentance is the only thing that changes the way we act. It is not just telling God we're sorry and asking His forgiveness – it is a shift in how we think, which transforms how we behave.

Before I repented and was spiritually reborn, I hid in the world. I identified with bad people. To fit in, I tried to be like them, secretly believing I was superior so I could feel good about myself. I hid because, deep inside, I feared failure and I feared success. Failure generated rejection, and success might require more than I wanted to give.

Now I see hiding for what it is – *SELFISHNESS.* I recognize the things I have hidden behind. When I feel insecure, I'm still tempted to use those things as a smokescreen so people won't see me. Here is a partial list. Can you relate to any of these?

- **INTELLECTUALISM/RELIGION** – talking without making a commitment, for the sake of impressing others.

- **ABILITIES/GIFTEDNESS** – finding identity in what I do rather than who God says I am.

- **SELF-PITY** – a victim mentality, pandering for sympathy, which makes us pathetic and detestable.

- **UNFORGIVENESS** – inability to release the past.

- **PROCRASTINATION/PERFECTIONISM** – waiting until conditions are perfect before moving ahead.

- **MAN-PLEASING** – changing who I am to meet the expectations of others and manipulate them.

- **CHURCH** – putting in an appearance to be seen by men without acknowledging my need for God.

- **MINISTRY** – using position as a front to impress rather than a platform to serve.

- **DUTY** – the Martha syndrome, "I'm doing my best for God," substituting works for a relationship with Him.

- **PERSONAL APPEARANCE** – if I rely on how I look (good or bad), people won't know the real me.

Chapter 4 – Where Do We Hide?

- **ENTERTAINMENT** – making life about gratifying myself rather than pleasing God.

- **RESISTING/STUBBORNNESS** – the opposite of being humble and teachable.

STUBBORNNESS

When God teaches us, He doesn't want to merely add to our libraries of knowledge; He wants to change our hearts. I have intellectualized many things I should have internalized. Without realizing it, I tried to use that knowledge to influence others rather than become more Christlike. That is another form of hiding.

It scared me when I read in I Samuel 15:23, **"For rebellion is as the sin of witchcraft, and stubbornness is as iniquity and idolatry."** I recognized stubbornness in myself as a passive attempt at manipulation. That Scripture equates stubbornness to idol worship and puts it in the same reference as witchcraft.

God told Barbara and me that witchcraft does not have to be performed by witches. Usually, He said, it is when a person with unforgiveness is trying to manipulate others:

"Witchcraft is not just spells and potions. My Word says it is rebellion, and rebellion is always against authority. So when trying to identify where witchcraft comes against you, don't just consider nameless, faceless people who oppose your beliefs. Look at the people under your authority. Even if they are not consciously trying to undermine your authority, if they are using the techniques of rebellion and disobedience and disrespect, it accomplishes witchcraft."

Where Do You Hurt? Where Do You Hide?

BEING MISUNDERSTOOD

Hiding insulates us from relationships. It is pain management, a form of self-medication. One of the most convenient places to hide is in feeling misunderstood. There is something so unfair about it, far worse than being wrong. Our intentions are called into question; and usually, no amount of explanation can rectify the situation. This leads to more fear and hiding. The Lord taught us:

"Fear of being misunderstood, disregarded or embarrassed has to do with image. What if Jesus had those fears while He was on Earth? It would have cluttered the way to His destiny. When He made Himself of no reputation, He gave up the right to those fears.

"Jesus did not insist on being understood or acknowledged. He was the King of Glory, without palace or possessions. He had more power than anyone could imagine, but did not use it to make Himself look good. That's being unselfconscious.

"This is part of the burden of your cross. If you complain while you're carrying your cross, are you truly following Jesus?

"Being misunderstood is the hardest offense to get over because it makes you feel the most helpless. Wasn't Jesus misunderstood? And yet He chose not to take offense. Why? Because of love.

"Duty and proving yourself don't know that kind of love. Working hard and achieving results don't develop that kind of love, even when you labor to help other people.

Chapter 4 - Where Do We Hide?

Such love is an attitude of the heart, not an achievement of the hands. It overlooks offense, which is the real meaning of 'Love covers a multitude of sins.'"

DUTY

What a loaded word "duty" is. On the surface it suggests responsibility and faithfulness – visible qualities of obedience. Duty in itself is not a bad thing. How can it be a place to hide?

Duty does not require passion. We lose the vitality of a relationship with the Lord if devotion degenerates into duty. When obedience becomes mechanical and life is about us, not God, then duty is a place to hide rather than grow. Duty robs us of our zeal. We no longer love with abandon, live with joy, and trust without reservation. Even worship becomes a duty rather than a response to Him.

Joyless obedience causes the world to view our faith as little more than a belief system, not a vibrant bond with the Creator of the universe. Christianity is reduced to toeing the line and striving to get to heaven. Duty without devotion is, at best, self-satisfying and not an expression of loving God.

When duty is subject to a man-pleasing spirit, it says, "As long as I'm doing what's right, you won't see the real me and you can't criticize me," or, "I am a good servant, so you don't have the right to require anything else from me."

We can get stuck in duty, like the circus bear that continues to pace back and forth in his cage while the door is open and his trainer is coaxing him out.

The Lord told me, "Son, you hide in being responsible

Where Do You Hurt? Where Do You Hide?

(dutiful). While this is commendable because it is for My Kingdom, it becomes an idol if you put it ahead of Me."

HIDING BEHIND A VEIL

The veil is a barrier. Middle Eastern women wear it to hide their faces as a form of modesty. Imagine trying to hide from God behind a veil of religion. It sounds like a contradiction, but isn't the function of a religious spirit to separate us from God by legalism and tradition? With this religious spirit comes the unteachable nature of self-righteousness, **"having a form of godliness but denying its power"** (II Timothy 3:5). Paul wrote, **"from such people turn away!"**

After God spoke to Moses face to face as a man speaks with his friend, Moses wore a veil because the skin of his face shone. When a veil covers our hearts, it can prevent God's glory from impacting us. That veil can be distractions, fears, circumstances, daydreaming, rehearsing the future, living in the past – whatever we put ahead of the True and Living God.

Barbara and I lead devotions once a month in an area homeless shelter. We have ministered in similar environments for our whole life together. We've seen how disappointment and misunderstanding have beaten people down to survival level. It is hard for a man's spirit to seek God when his flesh is consumed with preserving itself. That is why the Lord instructed us, "Bring them out of hiding."

"ARISE, SHINE!"

In this season, we often hear Isaiah 60:1-3 quoted, **"Arise, shine; for your light has come! And the glory of the Lord is risen upon you. For behold, the darkness shall cover the earth,**

Chapter 4 – Where Do We Hide?

and deep darkness the people; but the Lord will arise over you, and His glory will be seen upon you. The Gentiles shall come to your light, and kings to the brightness of your rising."

The Lord told us this passage can be interpreted:

"Be joyful! For the season of God's favor upon you is beginning. The grace you have already enjoyed is being multiplied. God is filling you as never before, to send you out to represent His Kingdom so His banqueting hall will be full.

"This is the time He will reveal Himself through His children. They will bear His likeness, speak in His name, and produce much fruit of righteousness. Everyone will be drawn to them, from the mighty to the meek.

"His children's words will be His words, and they will walk in His authority. They will be bright, shining stars of light and love. And only those bound for destruction will be able to resist them."

This cannot happen if a veil hides our hearts from God, or hides His light on our faces from the world around us.

Chapter 5

Walking in the Light

Satan tempts us to *hide things we do* so we won't be forgiven and restored. He wants us in a downward spiral of trying to maintain secrets, agreeing with darkness, and living in fear that someone will discover those things and bring them into the light. God wants us to commit them to Him while the enemy wants us to think we can hide them from Him.

God said to Jeremiah, **"For My eyes are on all their ways; they are not hidden from My face, nor is their iniquity hidden from My eyes"** (Jeremiah 16:17). And Job wrote, **"There is no darkness or deep shadow where the workers of iniquity may hide themselves"** (Job 34:22 NASB).

Sin was birthed in deception and thrives by deception. In the Garden of Eden, the first act of disobedience resulted from deception, and it altered the course of humanity. But God already had a remedy, the Lamb slain from the foundation of the world, Jesus.

The real story of mankind is not one of deception and

disobedience, but one of redemption and restoration. The Lord told us:

"Redemption is My plan to release man from the bondage of constantly having to invent himself. I want to restore him as the creation I fashioned in the beginning.

"I AM the prodigal's Father, and My desire is to restore all My sons to their rightful place. So naturally, this is where the deceiver does most of his work. He wants you to believe that I will reject you so he can place his orphan spirit on you.

"It's really a choice this simple: Whose spirit do you want to receive, Satan's or Mine?"

THE ORPHAN SPIRIT

After listing many dangers faced by Christians of his day, Paul asks in Romans 8:35, **"Who** (not 'What') **shall separate us from the love of Christ?"** He is referring to Satan, whom Revelation 12:10 calls **"the accuser of our brethren, who accused them before our God day and night."**

Satan was once Lucifer, the **"star of the morning [lightbringer], son of the dawn"** (Isaiah 14:12 AMP). When he led a rebellion and was expelled with one-third of the angels, he fell **"like lightning from heaven"** (Luke 10:18) and became the first orphan. Now he tries to persuade men, "Your fate is the same as mine." He uses fear to convince us.

The orphan spirit operates in fear and makes its victim anxious about provision and protection. That person expects failure, rejection and abandonment. He feels out of place, unwanted, unappreciated and alone. He is insecure about relationships and avoids genuine intimacy. He has trouble trusting others and is leery of those in authority. He operates in a victim mentality and interprets disagreement or correction as disapproval and disrespect. He is critical, judgmental and condemning. Anger and poverty often accompany an orphan spirit.

The characteristics of the orphan spirit contradict God's promises to us, as in Philippians 4:6-7, **"Be anxious for nothing, but in everything by prayer and supplication, with thanksgiving, let your requests be made known to God; and the peace of God, which surpasses all understanding, will guard your hearts and minds through Christ Jesus."**

Hiding is a strategy Satan uses to make us feel distant from God so we expect nothing from Him. Then the orphan spirit has free reign in our lives. God sent His precious Son to purchase our forgiveness with His blood and secure our place in His family. It insults Him when we think and act as orphans.

MY LIFE AS AN ORPHAN

Satan tried to change my identity to that of an orphan who is overlooked, unloved, worthless. I saw myself as a non-person without a destiny. I simply existed, like water in a river, with no understanding of where I was going. Without a positive self-image to live up to, I did whatever came along. My life was rudderless, lacking aspiration and vision. It was painful to feel like an orphan.

People medicate emotional pain with whatever is at hand. For many it's drugs or alcohol. Others are abusive. Still others use work and personal ambition to distract themselves. And how about preoccupation with entertainment? They are all forms of hiding. Whenever we hide, we walk in darkness.

Jesus said in John 12:35, **"Walk while you have the light, lest darkness overtake you; he who walks in darkness does not know where he is going."** That darkness is the confusion Isaiah alluded to when he wrote, **"the darkness shall cover the earth, and deep darkness the people"** (60:2).

THE STRATEGY OF GUILT AND SHAME

I walked in that darkness, with no purpose except to please myself. *"How,"* you ask, *"did you ever come out of such a selfish lifestyle?"* Simple. Jesus called me. He altered the course of my thoughts until I could no longer resist Him.

As I was completing this book, Barbara and I were thanking God for the life He has given us and the remarkable grace He has provided. Barbara asked, "How did we ever get saved? It wasn't any goodness in us." The Lord replied:

"I take issue with that statement. Can you find Me a man about whom you can say with confidence, 'There is no goodness in him'? You wouldn't dare make such a judgment. Then why would you say it about yourself?

"The goodness in the worst of men might be overcome by evil, but I can still see it. That's why I call Myself 'the God of unlikely vessels.' My ways are not your ways. You judge by appearances and I judge by the heart.

"You should be greatly encouraged that I selected you to be one of My standard-bearers. I can completely forgive all your mistakes because you are Mine.

Where Do You Hurt? Where Do You Hide?

"Not everyone will come to Me on this basis. Even people who are aware of Me can allow their past to be a barrier to the future I desire for them.

"The enemy of your soul brings up the past in his accusations to keep you stuck in regrets so you will not move forward. But grace is more powerful than condemnation, and I offer it freely so people will see I AM more powerful than sin.

"Forgiveness is one of the greatest forces in the universe. I AM willing to forgive men, but they must be willing to forgive themselves. The strategy of guilt and shame is designed to keep men from forgiveness. That's why I sent My Son."

"DARKNESS HAS NOT OVERCOME IT"

When I was lost, the light of people who told me about God's love and the sacrifice of Jesus was more powerful than the darkness I walked in, and my darkness could not extinguish it. That light proved so irresistible that even the shame which provoked me to hide was forced to yield to it.

In my journalism career, before the advent of digital photography, I learned to develop film and print photos. While setting up darkrooms, I discovered several enduring principles about light:

1. It is nearly impossible to seal all light out of a room.

2. The longer I was in the dark, the brighter an invading ray of light appeared.

3. When I opened the door, darkness did not spill out

Chapter 5 - Walking in the Light

and overcome the light; rather, light came in and
dispelled the darkness.

**"The light shines in the darkness, and the darkness has
not overcome it"** (John 1:5 ESV).

SHAME PRODUCES HIDING

We think the enemy wants to make us sin. He really
wants to make us ashamed, and sin is the way he does it.
Shame produces hiding and separates us from God.

**"But if we walk in the light as He is in the light, we have
fellowship with one another** (with God)**, and the blood of
Jesus Christ His Son cleanses us from all sin"** (I John 1:7).

When I remember the arrogance of disregarding people's feelings while only being interested in my own lusts, I
am still tempted to embrace shame. I had the total conceit
to do things at the expense of others without thinking twice
about it, and I had the nerve to believe I could get away with
it. But God has helped me overcome the shame I carried
since my childhood. One way He has done that is with a
deeper understanding of the whole armor of God.

WALKING IN THE LIGHT: GOD'S ARMOR

Barbara has seen the armor as God's glory, shimmering
because it is alive, covering us just as it once covered Adam
and Eve. Barbara received the revelation that the Bible pres-
ents God's armor in a deliberate order. Here is her account:

"I had two dreams in a row where I saw my armor sitting
in the corner, on the floor. I realized I had not put it on in a
long time. So I started at the top by putting on the helmet of

salvation, working down to having my feet shod with the preparation of the Gospel of Peace, just as I once taught in children's church and Sunday school.

"After the second dream, I thought I should read it in Ephesians 6:14-17. I realized I was putting on the armor in the wrong order because there is significance to the sequence of every list in Scripture. The belt of truth comes first. I had a revelation that we cannot wear the breastplate of righteousness without first knowing the truth. Then, if we live righteously, we have peace, which causes us to walk in faith (our shield). Faith is required before we can wear the helmet of salvation and wield the Sword of the Spirit."

Putting on the whole armor of God is more than a prophetic act; it is covering ourselves with His glory. It symbolizes walking in obedience to His authority, and provides protection and empowerment.

REDEMPTION AND RESTORATION

Being covered with God's armor is an act of redemption and restoration. It repels the orphan spirit and frees us to trust God. It is a way to receive the eternal, unshakable peace Jesus promised us on His way to the cross, when He said, **"Peace I leave with you, My peace I give to you; not as the world gives do I give to you. Let not your heart be troubled, neither let it be afraid"** (John 14:27).

The Lord told us:

"When there is no peace, there is always blaming. Do you believe you can have peace no matter what anyone says or does to you? If it is no longer you who live but I live

Chapter 5 - Walking in the Light

in you, then it is no longer you who are insulted, and there is no reason for you to take offense. It's only when you have to defend yourself that people become enemies. That's when living deteriorates to survival.

"Peace and favor go hand in hand. Being a carrier of peace shows favor to those around you; and as you do to them, it is done to you.

"You can see how blaming spoils everything. It makes life a struggle. That's why it was so important that I gave My peace – which overcame every obstacle to My obedience – to those who follow Me.

"You know you are commissioned to take the Gospel and make disciples. How effective can you be without peace? In the world, you are just one more voice clamoring to be right if you lack peace. But when you possess true peace, people will want to hear what you have to say."

PUTTING PAIN TO WORK

Let your pain prompt you to pray for people around you. We are given this pain and suffering to cultivate generosity of spirit and pray for others, not just ourselves.

It's easy to learn how to pray beyond your personal needs. The world is full of reminders. When you see a school bus, pray for the safety of the students, driver and those in traffic around them. Pray for safety in the schools and wisdom for the board of education as they determine policies and curricula.

When you hear a fire siren, yield to an ambulance, or

see a medevac helicopter, speak life to the situation. Pray for safety. Pray for wisdom, skill, understanding, knowledge, insight and discernment for anyone rendering medical aid. And pray for the salvation of each person involved.

When Barbara and I approach the signs at the city limits of our regional center of influence and supply, they remind us to pray for every aspect of life within its borders.

Highways, police cars, government facilities, military installations, newscasts and so many more things we see every week can prompt us to pray, if we're open to it. This will not happen if we are hiding, even if we're hiding in plain sight.

Christianity is like a contact sport. But many Christians wear the uniform without ever getting it soiled because they are not in the game. Resembling spectators, they only watch. It's better to get dirty or even hurt while engaged, rather than sit on the sidelines and warm the bench.

Wearing the jersey of our favorite sports franchise shows support, but it doesn't mean we're on the team.

Chapter 6

The Truth That Makes Us Free

For me, hiding evidenced the larger need to place my whole confidence in God, and trust Him in everything. *"How did you come out of hiding?"* you might ask.

God has shown me how many of the things I've written and taught were platitudes that did not become my personal convictions. He revealed these eternal truths to me for my own growth, to learn for myself before I preached them to others. If I embraced them intellectually without applying them to my own life, I was a hypocrite, not practicing what I preached.

So God pulled me out of the lecture hall, where these concepts are simply discussed; and put me into the laboratory, where they must be proven in a hands-on environment. He started one year ago by calling them to my mind one by one, then asking, **"Do you *really* believe that? Do you believe** it enough that you're willing to experience it and trust Me through it?"

As the Author and Finisher of my faith, He is testing me for my benefit. These concepts are basic tenets of the Christian life which I thought I was already doing, such as:

- We walk by faith and not by sight.

- God is our source, not wealth, government or other people.

- God loves us with an everlasting love which does not depend on our works.

- Fear not.

- Suffering promotes our spiritual maturity.

- Seek God's Kingdom first and He will supply all our needs.

- Pray with gratitude and God's peace will protect us.

- Trust in the Lord with all our hearts, not our intellect, and He will direct us.

TRUTH

God tempts no man to sin, but He tests us to produce greater faith. Spiritual growth spurts come in ranks, like grade levels in school. If we want to move on to the next one, we have to pass the quizzes, tests and a final exam. We don't want to just cram the night before a test; we want to learn the material that prepares us for the next grade.

Now, 33 years after the day of my salvation, God has me

Chapter 6 - The Truth That Makes Us Free

examining myself to see if my Christianity has been a lifestyle or only a label. II Corinthians 13:5 says, **"Examine yourselves as to whether you are in the faith."** Do my beliefs constitute abundant life or mere a philosophy? Am I a real disciple who is being freed by the truth, or have I traded on truth as the scribes and Pharisees did to ensure their position? We should all ask ourselves these questions.

Jesus told His followers in John 8:31-32 (GW), **"If you live by what I say, you are truly My disciples. You will know the truth, and the truth will set you free."** He didn't say, "If you preach My Word," but, "If you live by what I say."

God has ordained a season when everything I thought I believed is coming up for review, to drive the truth down into the depth of my being. **"Behold, You desire truth in the inward parts, and in the hidden part You will make me to know wisdom"** (Psalm 51:6).

Relating the truth without living it does not make it any less true. But Jesus said *doing* the truth brings us into the light (and out of hiding), so we will clearly demonstrate that our works have been done by God's power and not in our own strength (John 3:21). God wants me – and all of us – to **"be *doers* of the Word, and not *hearers* only, deceiving yourselves"** (James 1:22, emphasis added).

Seasons of testing will arouse our emotions, but we can't let feelings interfere with the understanding that God has our best interests at heart. He said to me:

"You cannot depend on your feelings. You must stand only on My Word because only My Word does not fail.

Where Do You Hurt? Where Do You Hide?

"You know My Word – put it to work for you. Unless you exercise it (that means not just read it but live by it), you are a hearer and not a doer. I tell you this not to condemn you nor dash your hope, but in My love to exhort you to receive from Me all that I have for you.

"IN THE DAYS AHEAD, YOU CANNOT STAY IN YOUR ROWBOAT. YOU WILL NEED AN ARK. The next rain I bring upon the face of the earth will be fire and Spirit at the same time.

"Judgment and revival will flood the planet, just as when Noah escaped the deluge. Unless Noah had been obedient to Me, he would not have survived. I AM telling you to do the same thing. Exercise My Word."

GOD'S RESPONSE

God requires us to take Him at His Word, just as He takes us at ours. I believe my season of testing and faith-building is in response to the "Transition Prayer" God told us to pray many years ago. We still pray this frequently:

"Father, prepare us for transition. Remove what is dead and prune what remains, that we will bring forth more fruit."

When the Lord suggested that Barbara and I "soak" in His presence every day, we weren't sure what He meant. He told us to sit quietly and focus on Him, and He would do spiritual surgery on us. That encouraged us, so we didn't think we had failed when our minds wandered or we fell asleep.

We try to do this twice daily, with instrumental music in

the background, for anywhere from 10 minutes to sometimes an hour. Knowing it isn't a waste of time has become a great joy. My season of testing is God's response to this prayer He told us to say each time we soak:

"We commit our beings to the grace and authority of God Almighty, and request You to work on us as we sit still. Perfect us as saints. Instill in us Your attributes. Enlarge our capacities for faith. Make us productive fruitbearers for Your Spirit. Rest Your peace in us so our eyes will always be on You. And teach us the joy of Your salvation."

I can see how this testing is "removing what is dead and pruning what remains." God is using it to "enlarge my capacity for faith" and "rest His peace in me." He has rocked my world and shaken many things that could be shaken. By compelling me to acknowledge what I believe, He is revealing my salvation as a process of coming out of hiding.

As faith and trust grow in me, I'm rediscovering the way I loved Jesus when I was first saved. It had nothing to do with my circumstances; no matter what they were, I wasn't worried. I was totally enraptured with and dependent on Jesus. I am returning to my first love, where my eye is not on my situation but on His faithfulness.

FACTS AND TRUTH

Truth exists on its own merit, regardless of whether it is presented by someone who lives by it. Facts, on the other hand, can change. One day, it's hot; the next, it's cold. One day, I feel good; the next, I feel lousy. Facts aren't necessarily truth. Eternal truth never changes.

Where Do You Hurt? Where Do You Hide?

My tendency has been to live out of my soul and not my spirit. This season is forcing me to sort out intellectual (soulish) facts from eternal (spiritual) truth. Here are some of the truths I am grasping:

- I am connecting truth with faith, so I can internalize them on a deeper level.

- When challenges take me by surprise, truth reminds me that God has my best interests at heart.

- To fully enter my new season and receive my upgrade, there are things I can't take with me from my old season.

- Many times when I thought I had peace, I was merely comfortable. Now I'm learning to tell the difference.

- Giving up the security of the familiar produces either trust or fear; I want to choose trust.

- Transition is disconcerting, and pruning is painful.

- The end-product of refinement will be beneficial.

I try to declare this every day:

"Father God, I am a son in Your Kingdom. I trust You to provide my needs because You have my best interests at heart. I accept where You have me and trust where You are taking me. I want to please You with faith and position myself for what You want to do. I need Your help to do this."

FEAR IS OF THE ENEMY

All fears come from the fear that "God does not love me." The enemy tries to convince us of that with shame, false guilt and a sense of unworthiness. He does not want us to know the truth written by John in his first epistle, **"God is love"** (I John 4:8). No other passage in Scripture captures God's nature so completely and succinctly.

Satan, our accuser, wants us to believe God's love must be earned, that He operates on a merit system, and the requirements are out of our reach. He wants us to think we will never qualify, that we have no hope, that our Father in heaven has given up on us.

That is so contrary to God's nature. During our prayer time, He told us:

"You still don't know how much I value you, because you think it's in response to what you do. Do you really think you can impress Me?

"When you understand My love better, you'll see there is no need to try and win My favor. Then you will want to please Me out of love for Me and not love for yourself."

LOVE FOR OTHERS

As God's Kingdom ambassadors to this world, we are to reflect His nature. Ambassadors do not have their own agenda. They precisely represent the wishes and policies of the head of state who sends them. So when God tells us to love people, He wants us to share the love He has given to us, and use it to reveal Him to others.

The Lord taught us this about His love:

"Love is something I give you, and not something you work up. Before others can receive your love, you must

receive Mine.

"You receive My love by trusting Me and watching Me work in your life. Then, when you know you are loved with a perfect love, your love will be perfected.

"It's important that you start remembering to trust Me in everything, not from the mind or lips but with your whole heart. That means giving up your rights to be angry or hurt, to feel bad about yourself, or to be right. When you don't depend on those things but depend on Me, trusting and loving will be much easier. Then you will see that trusting Me and loving others are really the very same thing."

Chapter 7

Assignments and Authority

"What does it feel like to stop hiding?" It hasn't made me insecure. I feel relieved and released to be my real self. The only areas which still make me nervous are those in which I haven't learned to trust God with my heart instead of my lips.

I have had to repent of:

- Double-mindedness – saying, "I trust God," while thinking, "I have to do this my way."

- Preaching truth to others but not always doing the truth myself.

- Wearing Jesus' name like a badge to make me look good and give me influence.

- Hiding behind a façade of religion while concealing doubts and fears.

- Believing God's desire was to make me comfortable rather than increase my faith.

Where Do You Hurt? Where Do You Hide?

• Self-righteously judging others when I should have shown compassion.

My repentance has been more of a process than an event. It has been a deep work that takes place in layers: Each time one is peeled off the top, another rises to the surface.

"TOWN CRIERS OF REPENTANCE"

Coming out of hiding has made it easier to embrace assignments and authority from the Lord.

When my days with the *Manna* newspaper were drawing to a close, God transitioned Barbara and me into new ministry adventures. He told us, "You will speak about revival, but you will be town criers of repentance."

The Lord often has to remind us of what He said. We speak a lot about "revival," but talking about "repentance" has come more slowly. Perhaps it is because we are still comprehending repentance, which is God's desire for every man.

We learned about and started teaching strategic intercession – using prayer as a weapon of spiritual warfare. This employs tactics much as a military commander would use to take ground in a battle. After reconnaissance to determine the enemy's strengths and weaknesses and assess the terrain, an attack is launched, sending superior forces to where the enemy is most vulnerable.

We carry out our spiritual attacks using prayer, declaring the blood and sovereignty of Jesus, praising, worshiping, and performing prophetic acts. We declare God's Word, which does not return to Him void but accomplishes what He sends it forth to do (Isaiah 55:11), and will never pass away (Luke 21:33).

Chapter 7 - Assignments and Authority

DRIVE-BY SHOOTERS

We love this example of strategic intercession: In Baltimore, a team of three "mothers of the church" chose to do a drive-by shooting instead of a prayer walk, which would have been too difficult for them. Each was over 65 and more than 300 pounds.

They inquired at a police station where the precinct's most violent crime areas were, informing the officers they intended to pray at these hot spots, fully expecting to make a difference. At each location, they proclaimed the Word of God, prayed for change, and squirted anointing oil out of mustard bottles onto the ground. They declared, "Jesus Christ is Lord" – never getting out of their vehicle.

Returning to the police station six months later, they were told that crime at these hot spots dropped 50 percent since they prayed. An excited major asked them to pray at additional locations. Like these "mothers," we can all discover creative ways of obedience.

"PRAY FOR THE BAY"

In 2007, God assigned Barbara and me to pray for repentance in the Chesapeake Bay region. He said to do this from Tangier Island, which is located in the middle of the bay.

Tangier is strategic due to the phenomenal Methodist camp meetings which started there in 1807 and drew thousands from around the bay as part of the Second Great Awakening. The islanders' spiritual heritage gives them great authority in prayer.

Two hundred years later, because of the spiritual

outpouring which occurred there, the Lord told us Tangier is "the pearl in the oyster."

We named our campaign "Pray for the Bay." It wasn't an ecological initiative but a crusade for repentance of the (then) 17 million souls which lived around the Chesapeake. (A more complete account of "Pray for the Bay" appears in our book *Things Hoped For.*)

The Lord instructed us to "pray for the land ahead of the people, for the land is more cursed than the people are." He explained that curses on the land keep people in bondage and hinder them from being saved.

Sin defiles the land. As a result of sin, God said to Adam, **"The ground is [now] under a curse because of you"** (Genesis 3:17 AMP). Sin has brought curses to the land ever since.

God loves us and He loves the land. He wants to heal the land from the stain of iniquity. II Chronicles 7:14 says this will happen when men repent: **"If My people who are called by My name will humble themselves, and pray and seek My face, and turn from their wicked ways, then I will hear from heaven, and will forgive their sin and heal their land."** God wants the land healed so we can be set free to prosper. This comes through repentance.

THE HARVEST

After mobilizing a prayer network, we assembled 43 intercessors from around the east coast, and sailed to Tangier. On the water, we lifted up extravagant praise and worship, and took Communion. Our praises to God were so exuberant that the islanders said they could hear us coming.

Chapter 7 - Assignments and Authority

We prayed with Tangier residents for repentance and revival around the bay. On the return trip, the Lord instructed us to declare to the water, "Revival to the shellfish!"

Ecologists, government agencies and the media had all sounded the death knells of the bay. They said the water was so polluted that the famous Chesapeake Bay blue crabs were dying out, the oysters were dying out, and commercial fishermen would have to find another way to earn a living.

Eleven days after we went to the island, Tangier's mayor called to say the bay floor was "crawling with crabs" in the area where we prayed. It was a harbinger of the largest crab harvest in living memory, both in quantity and size of the crabs. Watermen caught so many that their shanties weren't large enough to hold them. When the crab season ended, the oysters returned and each waterman caught his limit.

Barbara and I asked the Lord what this miraculous sign meant, and He said, *"If you can speak it to the shellfish, you can speak it to the people."*

The harvest has been continuing and expanding in the eight years since. The water itself has become mysteriously more clear. "We've got water like you'd see in the Caribbean," the mayor told *The Virginia-Pilot* in November, 2015.

After "Pray for the Bay," we interceded at hundreds of places around the bay's 5,700 miles of shoreline, praying for repentance, revival and healing of the land. Our goal was to add our prayers to those of faithful intercessors who have gone before, and fill the bowls of heaven to the tipping point. Sometimes we were joined by others. Many times, it was just Barbara and myself.

Where Do You Hurt? Where Do You Hide?

OPPOSING A SPIRIT OF DEATH

After a season of having us intercede around the bay and in Washington, D.C., the Lord assigned Barbara and me in 2009 to pray for the City of Salisbury, Maryland, our region's center of influence and supply. He specifically told us to "oppose a spirit of death" there. This small city of about 35,000 people was identified as the fourth most dangerous for its size in the nation.

We started by praying at its four gates, naming them **Truth, Holiness, Justice** and **Peace**. From them we proclaimed blessings from Scripture over the city. We led prayer teams at strategic places, some of which were suggested by city leaders: schools, churches, government buildings, municipal facilities, crime hot spots and homeless camps. We gathered to pray specifically for backsliders, prodigals, fathers and families.

The campaign was called "A Time to Love Salisbury," and included 200 yard signs which declared, "Salisbury, It's God's Time for You. PRAY: Churches Come Together, Righteousness Prevail, Wells of Revival Flow." (A more complete account of the Salisbury prayer campaign appears in our book *Things Hoped For.*)

Barbara and I repented at the courthouse for a 1931 lynching on its lawn, and the racism which provoked it. We prayed with university students for revival on their campus. We asked the mayor and chief of police how to pray for Salisbury. We attended city council meetings as silent intercessors, and enrolled in the Citizen's Police Academy to learn how to better pray for law enforcement.

Chapter 7 - Assignments and Authority

I met with area pastors and asked them what they thought revival would look like in the city, and what God's vision for Salisbury was. It was obvious by their responses that this enlarged their thinking beyond the weekly requirements of building and property maintenance, visiting parishioners, church programs and preparing their next sermon.

Chartering a school bus, we organized two "Freedom Rides" around Salisbury. In one, intercessors praised and prayed a protective wall of righteousness along its borders. For the other, we prayed on the grounds of all 32 public schools and colleges in and around the city. And Barbara and I led a time of community intercession during the regional prayer breakfast on the National Day of Prayer.

As prayers for Salisbury were having an effect, the chief of police and state's attorney convened meetings of church leaders to share prayer requests from the law enforcement community. The chief of police specifically credited our intercession campaign with helping decrease violent crime in Salisbury, which was eventually reduced by 50 percent.

DISTURBING THE FORCES OF DARKNESS

While Barbara and I were praying for Salisbury, the quiet little street we live on was having problems of its own. One of the county's largest drug busts occurred next door to us. Down the street, a man would threaten to kill people whenever he was intoxicated. Another man was arrested for possession of child pornography. And up our street, a Christian man was struggling with what he viewed on his computer. We needed to intervene through prayer.

Where Do You Hurt? Where Do You Hide?

After taking Communion, we prayer-walked our street, stopping to pray and take Communion again at each house of offense. The language coming through the windows of one house told us we were disturbing the forces of darkness.

At the head of our street is the town's war memorial. We took Communion, anointed it and prayed. Then we asked God what this gate was called. Anticipating a name like those of the Salisbury gates, we were shocked when He replied, *"The name of this gate is Perversion... until you change it."* We realized that *if we don't name our gates, someone else will.*

We repeated the procedure and then asked the Lord what we should call the gate. *"Journey,"* He said. *"Call everyone on your street onto the journey into the Kingdom of God, or pray them off."* Within a couple months, at least four people either moved or were removed. We have to believe those who remain will come into God's Kingdom.

WE ALL HAVE ASSIGNMENTS

When Barbara and I drive up our peninsula toward the Chesapeake Bay Bridge, we pray at every bridge and body of water along the way. They all empty into the bay, so we declare them living waters which will bring cleansing to the bay and spiritual awakening to the residents around it. We continue to proclaim revival to the shellfish. We pray safety for bridges and important infrastructure located nearby. And we pray for the adjacent towns to experience transformation by an outpouring of God's Spirit. We declare the blood of Jesus and proclaim He is Sovereign Lord over the territory. There is no shortage of things, places and people to pray for.

Chapter 7 - Assignments and Authority

God did not form any of us by accident. He has a blueprint for our lives. Each of us is uniquely made (Psalm 139:14) and destined for His plans and purposes (Jeremiah 29:11).

Scripture contains three groupings of spiritual gifts given to men for God's special assignments. Romans 12:6-8 lists **prophesying, serving, teaching, encouraging, giving, ruling, and showing mercy.** We don't only possess these gifts, we are *gift persons* for the sake of those to whom we are sent.

I Corinthians 12:8-10 identifies **words of wisdom, words of knowledge, faith, healings, miracles, prophecy, spiritual discernment, speaking in tongues and interpretation of tongues.**

Ephesians 4:11-13 says Jesus gave **"some to be apostles, some prophets, some evangelists, and some pastors and teachers, for the equipping of the saints for the work of ministry, for the edifying of the Body of Christ, till we all come to the unity of the faith and of the knowledge of the Son of God..."**

Each of us needs to seek God's instructions for our specific assignments. When Barbara asked the Lord how we should pray for America, He responded:

"First, ask forgiveness on behalf of the nation. Pray for understanding because you can't repent without it. Don't pray issues, pray for hearts. Altered behavior does not last unless the heart itself is transformed.

"Ordain a release of faith. Declare Christians will walk in and display righteousness. Call for an end to the famine of My Word by declaring hunger for truth. Call for a generation of peacemakers, not compromisers. And don't forget to pray for the land.

Where Do You Hurt? Where Do You Hide?

"When you rend heaven (with prayer), you amplify confusion and fear in the enemy camp. This is spiritual warfare at its most powerful. Then you can pray that your enemies' plans and devices be dismantled. Pray for a release of truth to them (so they are saved).

"Your enemies are in bondage, so they seek to put you in bondage. Declare truth that sets them free, and the coals of fire upon their heads will become a helmet of salvation."

DO I MAKE A DIFFERENCE?

God loves you, and He doesn't want you to hide from Him. You will never be more fulfilled than when you do what He created you for.

God is **"not willing that any should perish, but that all should come to repentance"** (II Peter 3:9). Part of repentance is coming out of hiding. God has given believers **"the ministry of reconciliation"** (II Corinthians 5:18) to bring others out of hiding too. He wants to reconcile the world to Himself.

We are commanded to pray, even while we await God's individual instructions to us. Don't pass the buck. God told the prophet in Ezekiel 22:30, **"I sought for a man among them who would make a wall, and stand in the gap before Me on behalf of the land, that I should not destroy it; but I found no one."**

How sad. Will you be one He can count on to pray?

Matthew Henry's Commentary says of this passage, "Sin makes a gap in the hedge of protection that is about a people at which good things run out from them and evil things pour in upon them, a gap by which God enters to destroy them. There is a way of standing in the gap, and making up the breach against the judgments of God, by repentance, and prayer, and reformation. Moses stood in the gap when he made intercession for Israel to turn away the wrath of God... When God is coming forth against a sinful people to destroy them He expects some to intercede for them, and enquires if there be but one that does; so much is it His desire and delight to show mercy."

There have been times when Barbara and I didn't feel like doing our assignment. Our first prayer outing in Salisbury was in a blizzard. We gave our word; we had to show up. Twelve intercessors braved the fast-accumulating snow to pray at the city's gates with us. This started the breakthrough which God told us to pursue until we see transformation.

WAITING ON GOD

People who think they are waiting on God may be using that as an excuse to hide from their calling. Another form of hiding is blame shifting.

When a friend of ours recognized someone else's shortcoming, she smugly asked the Lord, "Do *I* do that?" He answered, "Wrong question. Ask, '*How* do I do that?'"

To make sure we have not veered from God's path for us, Barbara asked Him, "Are we doing what we are called and made to do? He answered:

"What you're really asking is, 'Does my presence in the world make a difference?'

"How many lives have you touched? Thousands and thousands. You gave your witness by word and action. Their lives are different because of it.

Where Do You Hurt? Where Do You Hide?

"It's not only what you've done but what you represent. You demonstrate that it is possible to live a life for Me."

To complete that assignment, we must all ask ourselves, *"Where do I hurt, and where do I hide?"*

PRAYER

Heavenly Father, rescue me from the hidden hurts I carry. Expose them, help me overcome them, and set me free.

Reveal how and where I hide, and help me repent of it. Forgive me for trying to hide myself and what I do from Your love and goodness. Forgive me for hiding from my calling, wearing Your name without displaying Your nature, and hiding my light when the world is in darkness.

Show me whenever I try to hide by acting as the world does, thinking like an orphan, trusting in my strength instead of Yours, and most of all, failing to put my whole confidence in You.

Father, forgive me for not praying, not conducting Your assignments with my whole heart, not using my spiritual gifts for Your Kingdom purposes, and not embracing the authority You give me. Help me love others with Your love, and bring them out of hiding.

Cause resurrection life to flow into my dead places, and the blood of Jesus to cleanse me from fear that You don't love me. And help me always remember that You have my best interests at heart.

In Jesus' name, amen.